CONTENTS

REVENGE KILLINGS
CHRIS DORNER

The Cop. The Serial Killer. The Manhunt.

by RJ Parker

ISBN-13: 1522879312

ISBN-10: 1522879315

Copyright and Published

by

RJ Parker Publishing, Inc.

http://RJParkerPublishing.com/

Copyrights

Book Links

AUDIOBOOKS at RJ Parker Publishing
http://rjparkerpublishing.com/audiobooks.html

Collection of **CRIMES CANADA** books on Amazon.
http://www.crimescanada.com/

TRUE CRIME Books by RJ Parker Publishing on Amazon.
http://rjpp.ca/TRUECRIME-RJPP-BOOKS

ACTION/FICTION Books by Bernard DeLeo on Amazon.
http://bit.ly/BERNARD-DELEO-BOOKS

RJ Parker Publishing

Follow on *BookBub*

INTRODUCTION

What Happened and Why

Dorner was a former LAPD officer and was honorably discharged as a Naval reservist before he was accused of killing four people in February of 2013. The police claimed that Dorner was the author of numerous versions of a rage-filled Facebook note that later went on to become his manifesto.

In the note, Dorner had vowed to bring unconventional and asymmetrical warfare to those in a LAPD uniform, no matter if they were on duty or not. Later, Dorner was quoted in a local LA newspaper of saying that he didn't want to hurt anyone but only wanted to clear his own name.

After his death or what people are calling his supposed death, speculations are arising as to whether Dorner really was the domestic terrorist he was being portrayed as or if he was someone much less scary.

A sincere lack of evidence is the first thing that is raising alarms with a lot of people. The only pieces of evidence that can be found are ones that would arouse speculation at best. Until now, there have been sightings of people who look like Dorner who have killed people. As well, a photo of a .308 sniper rifle and a handgun has emerged, but these weapons were not used to connect Dorner with the murders since the modus operandi was majorly different from the ones that have been portrayed.

Additionally, there are multiple versions of the 'manifesto' circulating about the incident, but they are more related to the rights that the 2nd Amendment grants a person so that they can be called a terrorist as is being portrayed in modern day media. Most of the manifesto is based around Dorner's rather desperate attempts to clear his own name and not around killing people.

Additionally, apart from someone called Ronald Quan pretending to be Dorner, there is no evidence that Dorner himself had killed Monica Quan and her fiancé Keith Lawrence.

Another reason why the internet is in an uproar is over the fact that, despite this being the biggest manhunt for a single person since 9/11, we know very little about the case. The case involved FBI, SWAT teams, the services of over 10,000 police officers as well as tightened border patrol, especially in the Big Bear, California area. Furthermore, drones, helicopters and aerial teams with heat sensing technology were used, but they finally ended up having to roast Dorner in a cabin in Big Bear.

The interesting part is that usually charred corpses can be recognized via DNA or medical records or other means, but Dorner was recognized by his driver's license that was found near his burnt corpse in the basement of the cabin. A lot of people are claiming this to be absurd since the heat was so intense that it burnt the full cabin down and took Dorner with it, and hence the chances of a plastic identification card or a driver's license of surviving are almost nonexistent.

Furthermore, elements of the operation have caused Joe Citizen to raise eyebrows as well. In his own words, CBS correspondent John Miller who is also former head of the LAPD Major Crimes Unit, stated that:

"There was a remarkable bit of pre-staging involved in the crime scene." He said that the police were only keeping quiet in order to save and cover up the fact that they had let Dorner escape again. *"However, if Dorner really is still alive, it is interesting to note that he hasn't yet contacted the media as he was prone to do before the operation against him. Sources said that Dorner had cut off any and all electronic devices and ties he had on January 31. He realizes the fact that even the slightest bit of electronic activity would get him into trouble and would cause the authorities to come chasing after him yet again. Sources are also saying that the police is still on edge and is looking for any signs to jump on the fact that the body in the cabin was not in fact Dorner's body after all."*

Another reason for the raised suspicions is the fact that the LAPD blew the whole scenario way out of proportion.

Keeping in mind the fact that the LAPD is one of the most militarized police forces in America, one man's attempts to clear his name should not have sent the whole LAPD into the frenzy that it went into after Dorner's manifesto and statement came to light.

Los Angeles has its share of some of the world's most ruthless and well-armed crime rings. These include, The Crips, Bloods, Mexican Mafia, Yakuza, Armenian Mob, Aryan Brotherhood, Skinheads, and Russian mobs as well as the local drug cartels. These gangs are not only real, they are openly hostile towards the LAPD and have killed numerous police officers on numerous occasions.

Some of these gangs have even murdered entire families with the LAPD unable to catch them. Yet when an ex-cop, wanting to clear his name, tried to speak out against the LAPD, the police goes all out, 'balls to the wall', and embarked on one of the most organized and widespread manhunts in recent history.

Additionally, newer reports regarding Monica Quan have arisen that render an even greater air of speculation to the whole ordeal. Monica Quan and her fiancé, both with law enforcement backgrounds, were found in a car that was parked in a parking garage in a million-dollar predominantly white neighborhood. The parking garage was being guarded by a police officer who did not see Dorner, a large black man, break in. Additionally, the garages are monitored 24/7 and yet there is no footage of Dorner either breaking in, killing anyone, being there or leaving. Nothing. But that's what the LAPD wants people to believe.

All these scenarios separately might not mean much, but added together, they make the whole plot look like a poorly directed movie.

***

"I've heard many officers who state they see dead victims as ATVs, Waverunners, RVs and new clothes for their kids. Why would you shed a tear for them when they in return crack a smile for your loss because of the impending extra money they will receive in their next paycheck for sitting at your loved ones crime scene of 6 hours because of the overtime they will accrue. They take photos of your loved ones recently deceased bodies with their cellphones and play a game of who has the most graphic dead body of the night with officers from other divisions." [1]

In his manifesto, Christopher Dorner claimed that police officers had no compassion for the citizens they owed so much to. He alleged that the police were so desensitized that they did not care for the victims, instead disrespecting them by taking photos of gruesome crime scenes only to compare them later. He claimed that police officers didn't care about victims because they got paid overtime just to appear and remain at the crime scene.

"I never had the opportunity to have a family of my own, I'm terminating yours. Quan, Anderson, Evans, and BOR members look your wives/husbands and surviving children directly in the face and tell them the truth as to why your children are dead."

Dorner openly threatened the board that reviewed and investigated his case against Teresa Evans. Interestingly, he also suspected his own union representative Randal Quan of some sort of misconduct as well since he included him on the hit-list too.

BACKGROUND

Christopher Jordan Dorner was born on June 4, 1979 in New York, although he spent most of his childhood on the west coast in the South Californian Counties of Los Angeles and Orange County. Dorner stated, later on in his life, that he was the only African American student in his school from grades one through six and that he had gotten into multiple scuffles over his race.

He attended John F. Kennedy School in La Palma and Cypress High School in Cypress where he graduated in 1997. He went on to study Political Science (major) with a minor in Psychology. He subsequently graduated from Southern Utah University in 2001.

When he was a teenager, Dorner had already made the decision to become a police officer and embarked on his journey to do so by enrolling in a youth program offered by the La Palma Police Department.

It is worth noting that, at the time when the shootings occurred (the focus of this book), Dorner himself lived in La Palma. His neighbors described him as a son of an admired and amiable family though he usually kept to himself. Dorner was not married at the time of the shootings though he had been so previously. Court records state that his wife had filed for divorce early on in 2007. [2]

***

Christopher Dorner worked as a United States Navy Reserve Officer and was honorably discharged as a lieutenant in 2013. Commissioned in 2002, Dorner was commander of a Naval Security Unit at the Naval Air Station Fallon, Nevada.

Dorner also served with the Mobile Inshore Undersea Warfare Unit from June 2004 to February 2006. He was deployed to Bahrain with the Coastal Riverine Group Two from November 2006 to April 2007. He was discharged from the United States Naval Reserve in February of 2013.

Dorner joined the LAPD during his time serving at the Naval Reserve. He entered the academy in 2005 and graduated a year later in 2006. He started serving as a probationary police officer, but his duties were interrupted shortly after he started as he was deployed to Bahrain. Records show that on his return from Naval Reserve duty in July 2007, he was partnered with his LAPD training officer, Teresa Evans, in order to complete his probationary duty. According to the Los Angeles Times, Evans later stated that even on his first day working with her, Dorner had told her that he planned to sue the LAPD as soon as he had completed his probationary duties.

On July 28 of the same year, Dorner and Evans responded to reports of a disturbance that had taken place in the Doubletree Hotel in San Pedro where they found a disturbance being caused by a man named Christopher Gettler who suffered from dementia and schizophrenia. It was Gettler's arrest that marked the start of red notes appearing in Dorner's personnel file. After the arrest, Evans conducted a performance review of Dorner which indicated that he needed to improve in several areas. Immediately after this, Dorner filed a report stating that Evans had used excessive force in her handling of Gettler.

Dorner accused Evans of kicking Gettler in the face twice despite him being handcuffed and lying on the ground and therefore did not present any threat and hadn't resisted arrest.

This report caused the LAPD to launch an investigation that examined the report filed against Evans. The LAPD internal review board consisted of two LAPD captains as well as a criminal defense attorney. The investigation lasted seven months, during which Teresa Evans was assigned to desk duty and was forbidden to earn any money outside of her LAPD job. Dorner's representative attorney at the board hearing was a former LAPD captain named Randal Quan.

The review board was very thorough in its investigation and heard testimony from a good number of witnesses. These included three hotel employees who testified that they had witnessed most of the incident and had not seen the training officer manhandle the man, let alone kick him in any way.

Though Gettler had been brought in and had been treated for facial injuries post-arrest, he did not immediately mention being kicked in the face. However, later that day when Gettler was handed over to his father, he claimed that he had been kicked by an officer, a fact that his father testified to later at Dorner's disciplinary hearing.

In a videotaped interview with Dorner's attorney, Gettler said that he had been kicked in the face by a female police officer at the mentioned time and place. But when he was called to testify at the hearing, his replies to the board's questions are said to be noted as generally incoherent and non-responsive. The board concluded the investigation on the basis that there had been no kicking or excessive use of force and that Dorner had lied.

***

After the investigation, Dorner was fired by the LAPD due to making false accusations in his report as well as in his testimony against his training officer Teresa Evans. [3]

Dorner's attorney, Randal Quan, later stated that Dorner had been treated unfairly and had been used as a scapegoat just to protect the wrongdoings of a training officer.

Dorner later appealed his termination from the LAPD Board of Rights by filing a '*Writ of Mandamus*' with the Los Angeles County Supreme Court. The verdict was interesting, to say the least, as Judge David Yaffe wrote that he wasn't sure whether the training officer had actually kicked the suspect or not. However, he chose to uphold the department's decision regarding Dorner. Yaffe ruled that even though he himself was not certain whether Dorner's report regarding training Officer Evans was accurate or not, the LAPD board's investigation would hold merit and he, Yaffe, would be passing a verdict based on that.

This caused Dorner to actually cry out during the court proceedings in disbelief and he was recorded to have exclaimed, '*I was telling the truth! How could this happen?*' These words were later found to be repeated in Dorner's manifesto.

After this ruling, Dorner appealed to the California Court of Appeal to the Second Appellate District. The higher court upheld the lower court's ruling and affirmed it on October 3, 2011. According to California law, the administrative findings are entitled to be presumed as correct and the petitioner is supposed to bear the burden of proving that they are incorrect since Dorner could not provide substantial evidence.

Thus, the court ruled that the LAPD board of rights had passed the correct decision and its findings were true that Dorner had not been credible in his allegations against training officer Teresa Evans.

When his fellow colleagues were interviewed, many of them had only nice things to say about Dorner. Even though a lot of people claimed that they had never been especially close to Dorner, they said that he was a great person who put his morals and good nature above all else. They claimed that there was seldom a moment when Dorner had not been seen smiling.

However, a few other colleagues had less than polite things to say about Dorner. Some officers stated that Dorner had been one to use his race as leverage to pick fights, but there are no records of any fights being recorded involving Dorner, let alone fights that Dorner himself might have initiated.

THE DORNER MANIFESTO

It was early in February 2013 when Dorner posted a detailed note on his Facebook profile. This note coincided with what was only the start of a series of revenge shootings. In this note, Dorner discussed his history, his motivations, as well as his plans for the future. The note was around 11,000 words long and it became known later as the 'Dorner Manifesto'. [4]

Dorner's manifesto contained a list of around forty law enforcement personnel who he wanted to kill. Dorner stated that he knew that most of the people who know him personally would be in a state of shock and disbelief to hear that he was the suspect of committing such horrendous murders and having taken such drastic measures in the past few days.

However, he claimed that unfortunately he had been forced to act as what he described as the 'necessary evil' that he didn't enjoy but must partake in and complete for a substantial change to arise in the LAPD as well as in order to clear his name. He claimed that the department, far from getting better or changing since the 'Rampart Scandal' and 'Rodney King' days, had only gotten worse.

Dorner had just one demand: a public declaration by the LAPD that they had terminated him 'unfairly' simply because he had raised his voice and reported the use of excessive force. He urged journalists to pursue the 'fine truth' by pointing out some specific points from the investigation for reporters to follow under the Freedom of Information Act. He also claimed that he had dispatched video evidence to multiple news agencies.

On February 9, 2013, in response to Dorner's manifesto and the start of a murderous spree, LAPD Chief Charlie Beck assured Dorner through media that there would be a review of his case and the hearings that led to his dismissal. He assured Dorner that a full investigation would be launched by officials and his claims that his career was sabotaged by racist colleagues would be thoroughly examined.

Key Points Of The Manifesto

The manifesto was more an account of the happenings that had led him to the point where he thought that violence was his only option. The note contained some accounts of racial behavior toward Dorner that he had faced in his time working for different forces at different levels. [5]

In it, Dorner accused the LAPD of twisting

facts when it came to his case against Training Officer Teresa Evans, the final straw that led to his termination. The following are some excerpts from this 11,000 word note:

"Even with the multiple conversations and ambient noise I heard Officer Magana call an indivdual(sic) a nigger again. Now that I had confirmed it, I told Magana not to use that word again. I explained that it was a well known offensive word that should not be used by anyone. He replied, 'I'll say it when I want'." Officer Burdios, a friend of his, also stated that he would say 'nigger' when he wanted and never gave the word another thought.

"At that point I jumped over my front passenger seat and two other officers, then placed my hands around Burdios' neck and squeezed. I stated to Burdios don't fucking say that. At that point there was pushing and shoving and we were separated by several other officers. What I should have done, was put a Winchester Ranger SXT 9mm 147 grain bullet in his skull and Officer Magana's skull. The Situation would have been resolved effective, immediately."

This is the first sign in the manifesto where Dorner raises a point about officers using racial slurs that were offensive to him. He further pointed out that the officers continued to defiantly use the terms time and time again and even 'ganged up' against Dorner to ridicule him, a situation that only led him to violent acts.

In his manifesto, Dorner doesn't seem to be grieving over the fact that he reacted heatedly to the situation. Instead, he seemed sorry that he had not taken Officers Magana and Burdios's lives on the spot.

"The LAPD's actions have cost me my law enforcement career that began on 2/7/05 and ended on 1/2/09. They cost me my Naval career which started on 4/02 and ends on 2/13."

Dorner stated that it was the LAPD's actions that ended his short-lived career as a law enforcement official as well as his naval career. *"I've lost everything because the LAPD took my name and new [sic] I was INNOCENT!!! Capt Phil Tingirides, Justin Eisenberg, Martella, Randy Quan, and Sgt. Anderson all new [sic] I was innocent but decided to terminate me so they could continue Ofcr. Teresa Evans career. I know about the meeting between all of you where Evans attorney, Rico, confessed that she kicked Christopher Gettler (excessive force). Your day has come."*

Dorner also stated that he had lost everything he had because the LAPD had ruined his name despite the fact that he had been innocent. He went on, saying that the members of the investigative board were all aware that he was innocent but due to their desire to keep officer Teresa Evans's career intact, they acted against Dorner. He went so far as to say that Evans's attorney had confessed that she had kicked Gettler in the face but had chosen not to act upon that information.

"I'm not an aspiring rapper, I'm not a gang member, I'm not a dope dealer, I don't have multiple babies momma's. I am an American by choice, I am a son, I am a brother, I am a military service member, I am a man who has lost complete faith in the system, when the system betrayed, slandered, and libeled me. I lived a good life and though not a religious man I always stuck to my own personal code of ethics, ethos and always stuck to my shoreline and true North. I didn't need the US Navy to instill Honor, Courage, and Commitment in me but I thank them for re-enforcing it. It's in my DNA."

Here, Dorner allegedly claimed that he was being treated unfairly due to racial stereotypes. Dorner can be seen emphasizing the fact that he does not fit the stereotype that most people seem to have about dark-skinned people. He stated that he had always been a man of good judgment who valued his own code of ethics above all else and that the Navy hadn't drilled these values into his system but had only reinforced them.

"Self Preservation is no longer important to me. I do not fear death as I died long ago on 1/2/09. I was told by my mother that sometimes bad things happen to good people. I refuse to accept that."

It seems that long ago, before he tried to pin his thoughts down, Dorner had accepted the fact that his mission was a suicidal one. However, even knowing that no good would possibly come out of his plans, Dorner decided to go through with said arrangements in an attempt to fight back against fate and possibly the system in hopes of clearing his name and redeeming himself somehow.

"From 2/05 to 1/09 I saw some of the most vile things humans can inflict on others as a police officer in Los Angeles. Unfortunately, it wasn't in the streets of LA. It was in the confounds [sic] of LAPD police stations and shops (cruisers). The enemy combatants in LA are not the citizens and suspects, it's the police officers."

Again, we see hints of Dorner's allegations against the entirety of the LAPD of misdemeanors, especially treating the people they were supposed to be helping unfairly. He emphasized time and time again how the police were misusing and abusing their powers and targeting the people they should have been helping in the first place.

Time and time again in the manifesto, Dorner stated that all it would take for him to stop the killings would be for the LAPD to tell the people what the truth was and to clear his name from the false accusations that had been used against him.

"This department has not changed from the Daryl Gates and Mark Fuhrman days. Those officers are still employed and have all been promoted to Command staff and supervisory positions. I will correct this error. Are you aware that an officer (a rookie/probationer at the time) seen on the Rodney King videotape striking Mr. King multiple times with a baton on 3/3/91 is still employed by the LAPD and is now a Captain on the police department? Captain Rolando Solano is now the

commanding officer of a LAPD police station (West LA division). As a commanding officer, he is now responsible for over 200 officers. Do you trust him to enforce department policy and investigate use of force investigations on arrestees by his officers? Are you aware Evans has since been promoted to Sergeant after kicking Mr. Gettler in the face. Oh, you violated a citizens civil rights? We will promote you."

Dorner claimed that instead of dealing swift and crisp justice to the people who abuse their powers, the LAPD instead rewards them. He quoted multiple counts and cases where the officers who had been known to misuse and abuse their powers had been rewarded greatly for their misconduct instead of having been reprimanded and punished like they should have been. Quoting his own case, Dorner stated that as a reward for kicking Gettler in the face, training officer Teresa Evans had been promoted to the level of Sergeant. He claimed that even the officers who had video evidence against them of hitting, injuring and using excessive force against suspects had not only been let go free but had also been promoted to positions of great power with some of them being put in charge of hundreds of other officers. Dorner questioned what sort of a police force these officers who were excessively violent themselves would train for the near future.

"Those lesbian officers in supervising positions who go to work, day in day out, with the sole intent of attempting to prove your misandrist authority (not

feminism) to degrade male officers. You are a high value target."

Dorner started hinting at and naming victims blatantly throughout his manifesto. He claimed that racism wasn't the only problem with the police force. Female officers with a modicum of power used their power to commit acts of misandry against male officers. He claimed that anyone who freely abused their power was rewarded.

"Those of you who "go along to get along" have no backbone and destroy the foundation of courage. You are the enablers of those who are guilty of misconduct. You are just as guilty as those who break the code of ethics and oath you swore."

Dorner believed that the people who were unwilling to fight against the system and the misconduct and the abuse of powers by those above, below and around them had breached the code of ethics and the oath they had taken. In his eyes, they seem to be just as guilty as the abusers.

"I've heard many officers who state they see dead victims as ATVs, Waverunners, RVs and new clothes for their kids. Why would you shed a tear for them when they in return crack a smile for your loss because of the impending extra money they will receive in their next paycheck for sitting at your loved ones crime scene of 6 hours because of the overtime they will accrue. They take photos of your loved ones recently deceased bodies with their cellphones and play a game of who has the

most graphic dead body of the night with officers from other divisions."

In his manifesto, Dorner claimed that police officers had no compassion for the citizens they owed so much to. He alleged that the police were so desensitized that they did not care for the victims, instead disrespecting them by taking photos of gruesome crime scenes only to compare them later. He claimed that police officers didn't care about victims because they got paid overtime just to appear and remain at the crime scene.

"I never had the opportunity to have a family of my own, I'm terminating yours. Quan, Anderson, Evans, and BOR members Look your wives/husbands and surviving children directly in the face and tell them the truth as to why your children are dead."

Dorner openly threatened the board that reviewed his case and investigated his case against Evans. Interestingly, he also suspected his own representative Randal Quan of some sort of misconduct as well since he included him on the hit-list too. Another member of the list happened, typically, to be Teresa Evans.

"You said that I should have kept my mouth shut about another officer's misconduct. Maybe you were right. But I'm not built like others, it's not in my DNA and my history has always shown that. When you view the video of the suspect stating he was kicked by Evans, maybe you will see that I was a decent person after all. I

told the truth."

Dorner alleged that he had been told to keep quiet about the misconduct demeanor by his training officer Teresa Evans. He said that it was against his morals to twist the truth and pretend he had not seen what he had just to protect his own skin and his training officer.

Dorner's manifesto was a sort of action plan stating what he was going to do to the police officers. In various online postings, Dorner taunted Randal Quan after murdering his 28-year-old daughter Monica Quan. Allegedly, Dorner even called Quan in order to gloat over his daughter's death.

Dorner wrote in online postings that if anyone is to be blamed for the deaths, it is the culprits who ruined his career, are using the LAPD as a headquarters for their tyranny and are providing injustice in the name of justice. He said that if anyone was to be blamed for Monica Quan's death, it should be her father Randal Quan himself.

According to reports, a man claiming to be Christopher Dorner called Quan shortly after Monica's death had taken place but before her body had been discovered. Reports state that the man told Quan that he should have done a better job of protecting his own daughter. Shortly after this, the LAPD publicly pushed for Dorner to hand himself in for the first time. This appeal was accompanied by a

$1 million bounty for anyone who had any leads as to where Dorner was hiding.

LAPD Chief Charlie Beck said that, though the $1 million bounty had probably been one of the biggest ever offered in Southern California, it was remarkably easy to secure due to the fact that Dorner was proving to be such a security threat to law enforcement officials and their families in the region. A huge sum of the reward was raised by local police officers, businesses, communities as well as local governments across Southern California.

In a press conference held not long after the reward was announced, Los Angeles Mayor Antonio Villaraigosa announced that he would do all in his power to stop Dorner's 'reign of terror'.

When asked if he would approve the usage of 'drones' as had been used around the world in the 'war on terror', the mayor gave a very cryptic reply of, '*the police would be using all tools at their disposal in order to capture Dorner.*'

It is interesting to note that in his manifesto, Dorner had clearly stated that he had no qualms in coming in quietly, if only the LAPD would release the truth and, especially, release the video inter-view of Christopher Gettler in which he is clearly stating that he was kicked in the face by a female po-lice officer, who was training officer Teresa Evans.

However, it seemed that the LAPD had no de-sire to capture Dorner alive as was later established by the fact that on no less than two separate occasions, the police had opened fire on two passing cars simply because they fit the profile of the vehicle Dorner was supposed to have been driving.

In two separate incidents that took place in the early morning hours on February, 7, 2013, police opened fire on people who later turned out to be unrelated to Christopher Dorner in any way. Dorner was not even present at either scene when the shootings occurred.

The first incident took place at around 6:00 a.m. where at least seven LAPD officers, who were assigned to the protection of an unnamed LAPD official's residence in the Los Angeles County city of Torrance, opened fire at a passing light blue Toyota Tacoma.

There were two Hispanic occupants inside the car, Emma Hernandez, 71 and her daughter Margie Carranza, 47. The mother and daughter were delivering newspapers for the LA Times. Their vehicle, according to the police officers who had opened fire, was heading towards the home they were protecting, and had matched the description of Dorner's grey Nissan Titan and was moving without its headlights on.

Emma was shot in the back while Carranza suffered injuries to her hand. The attorney representing the women later stated that the police had no idea who was inside the vehicle. He said that there was nothing about his clients that remotely matched Dorner's profile, nor were their trucks even remotely similar. The two injured women later testified that the police had given them no warning prior to opening fire on their vehicle.

Further investigations revealed that the police had questioned Carranza's neighbors who stated that the two ladies delivered newspapers every single morning and that they always kept the headlights off so as to not disturb the neighbors in their sleep.

Later, the LAPD launched an internal investigation into the matter. The attorney for Hernandez and Carranza stated that their truck was riddled with 102 bullet holes.

Author's note: this clearly establishes the fact that the rules of engagement were to kill Dorner. I don't believe the LAPD had any intentions of taking him alive. My opinion will further be supported during the manhunt and cabin fire.

The LAPD has refused to comment on how many bullets were fired, how many holes were found, as well as how many police officers had been involved in shooting at the truck. It is also not mentioned if the two women were given any sort of verbal warning before firepower was opened up on them.

Later that year in April, the police paid a $4.2 million settlement to Emma Hernandez and Margie

Carranza, the two ladies who had suffered from bullet wounds at the hands of the police on the morning of February 7.

On the same day, less than half an hour after this incident took place, officers from the Torrance Police Department opened fire on yet another vehicle.

As in the first incident, officers involved in this shooting claimed that they had opened fire due to the similar resemblance of the vehicle in question to that of Christopher Dorner's truck. But later the vehicle was discovered to be a black Honda Ridgeline and the driver was found to be a white male.

The victim was David Perdue who was simply on his way to the beach in order to surf for a while before he went to work.

A Torrance Police Department cruiser smashed into Perdue's pickup before they opened fire on the vehicle. Fortunately, Perdue was not struck by any of the bullets. But he did suffer multiple injuries from the impact against his truck. The police later claimed that they had acted upon the similarities between the Perdue's and Dorner's vehicles. It was later confirmed by law enforcement that the vehicle was a different make and color than that of Dorner's.

A year after these incidents took place, on February 4, 2014, it was determined by the LAPD chief Charlie Beck that the police officers had in-deed used extensive and excessive force against the two women and Mr. Purdue. He said that the eight officers involved had violated the LAPD's use of force policy and that disciplinary action was being taken against them. California state law prevented him from disclosing the nature of the corrective action but that the punishment could range from ex-tended retraining up to termination. However, no criminal charges had been laid against any of these officers.

It is interesting to note that not long after these civilians had been shot at, online protest for-ums against the LAPD had popped up stating that they had great apprehensions against how Dorner were dismissed from the police service.

Furthermore, they had protested against how the police had a license to kill anyone they so pleased just because they thought that the victim looked like the suspect they had been pursuing.

TIME LINE

There are key events that took place during the Christopher Dorner debacle - the fired LAPD police officer who was suspected of having killed three people including a fellow police officer in Southern Carolina.

Dorner was said to have been working on his manifesto in which he had outlined plans to kill the police officers and their families who had, in some way or another wronged him, as well as their families.

- **Sunday, February 3** - assistant women's college basketball coach Monica Quan, 28, and her fiancé Keith Lawrence, 27, were found shot to death in a parked car in Irvine, California outside their condominium. Monica was the daughter of the former LAPD Captain and lawyer Randal Quan who had represented Dorner as an attorney in his case against then training officer, Teresa Evans, in front of an Internal Review Board who then fired Dorner.

- Dorner called Randal Quan shortly after

shooting his daughter and taunted him for not providing his daughter with better protection.

- **Monday, February 4** - some of Dorner's belongings as well as his police equipment were found in a trashcan in San Diego near the Irvine crime scene, thus linking him to the killings of Monica and Keith.

- **Wednesday, February 6** - the police first found Dorner's manifesto online, and he became suspect number one.

- A man matching Dorner's description made an attempt to steal a boat from a San Diego marina. The attempt was a failed one. An 81-year-old man was found tied up on the vessel that was meant to have been stolen, but otherwise he was unharmed.

- **Thursday, February 7** - around 1:30 am LAPD officers who were protecting an unknown person named in the manifesto chased a vehicle they believed was Dorner's. During the pursuit, one police officer was grazed in the forehead by a bullet but remained otherwise unscathed. The gunman escaped unidentified from the premises.

- On the same date a few hours later, a shooter believed to be Dorner ambushed two Riverside Police Officers who were doing a routine patrol. After a brief struggle, one officer lost his life whilst another was critically injured. Dorner escaped yet again.

- Again on the same date around 2:20 pm, a bus driver from a shuttle bus turned in a wallet with an LAPD badge and the picture identification of Christopher Dorner to the San Diego Police. The wallet was found less than five miles from the boat near the San Diego International Airport.

- 5:30 am on February 7, eight LAPD officers guarding another unknown manifesto target in the Los Angeles suburb of Torrance opened fire on a truck they believed to have belonged to Christopher Dorner. It was later found out that the truck was not even the same make and model as the one which Dorner drove. The occupants were a mother and daughter who were delivering newspapers. Both suffered gunshot wounds with the mother suffering a wound to her back and the daughter getting injured in the hand.

- Not long after the incident above, on the same date, the LAPD again opened fire and slammed a cruiser into another truck they believed to be similar to that of Dorner's. The passenger in the truck suffered minor injuries from impact but was not hurt otherwise.

- At 8:35 am, the police found a burnt-out pickup truck near the Big Bear ski area in the San Bernardino Mountains. The truck was examined and the authorities confirmed a few hours later that it was indeed Dorner's truck.

- At 9:40 am, the Naval Base Point Loma in San Diego was locked down after some Navy workers reported seeing some-one who resembled Christopher Dorner. Military officials later confirmed that Dorner had indeed checked into a hotel on the base earlier in the week, on a Tuesday, but had checked out shortly after on Wednesday. Dorner used a mili-tary ID to check in.

- Just after 4:00 pm the same day, author-ities searched a Las Vegas-area home that was said to have belonged to Dorner. They left with several boxes of items. The authorities later stated that no weapons had been found at the premises, but they still declined to comment as to what was discovered and taken away in the boxes.

- **Friday February 8**, dozens of searchers set out to hunt for Dorner in the freezing, snowy mountains of San Bernardino after they lost his footprints near the site where the truck had been found. Authorities had also searched Dorner's mother's house where they had collected ten bags of evidence and had also taken multiple electronic items for examination. The police also searched a storage locker in Buena Park.

- **Saturday February 9**, police helicopters used heat-seeking technology to search for Dorner in the mountains near Big Bear. Authorities later revealed that weapons and camping equipment was found in Dorner's burnt truck.

- **Sunday February 10**, the authorities announced a $1 million reward for any information leading to Dorner's arrest.

- **Monday February 11**, Riverside County Prosecutors issued a warrant charging Dorner with murdering a police officer and attempting to murder three other police officers in a case which punishment could potentially be a death penalty. Authorities had received more than 700 tips for Dorner's whereabouts since the reward had been announced.

- **Tuesday February 12**, police were alerted to a call after a man fitting Dorner's profile stole a vehicle in the San Bernardino Mountains. The vehicle was found rather quickly on Highway 38. After being found out, the suspect ran into the forest and barricaded himself inside a cabin.

- Twenty minutes later, the State Fish and Wildlife wardens were involved in a shoot-out with the suspect. During the cross-fire, two San Bernardino County Sheriff's deputies were wounded.

- Four hours later, police surrounded the cabin from all sides where the suspect was holed up. Gunfire erupted before the entire cabin caught on fire and law enforcement officials decided to wait for the fire to burn itself out.

- About thirty minutes later, a San Bernardino County Sheriff's spokeswoman confirmed that one of the two wounded deputies had died and the other was in surgery and was expected to survive.

The saga ended later that night around 6:30

pm when the police found a charred body in the rubble of the burnt cabin. Though they refrained from confirming the identity at the time, the police later confirmed that the body did indeed belong to Christopher Dorner.

INQUIRY

Shortly before Christopher Dorner's death on February 12, LAPD Chief Charlie Beck assured the public that they would reopen Dorner's case that led to his termination. He said that the purpose behind this was not to appease a murderer but in fact to reassure the public that the police department is transparent and fair in all that it does.

Numerous experts believed this to be a measure of damage control taken by the Chief of Police in order to avoid another riot like the ones that occurred in 1992 where people caused an uproar upon the emergence of a video tape showing white police officers beating a black man called Rodney King.

In explaining why he chose to reopen Dorner's case, the LAPD chief said, "*The LAPD has made tremendous strides in gaining the trust and confidence of the people we serve.*" He added, "*Dorner's actions may cause a pause in our increasingly positive relationship with the community.*"

To reiterate, Dorner joined the LAPD in 2005 and was fired in 2008 for giving false statements against his training officer Teresa Evans. He later went on to sue the department and lost the case as well as the appeal he made against it.

This decision to reopen the case was a significant turn-around from the stance the chief of police had shown a mere few days ago when he said that a trial or retrial simply wasn't possible. In his own words, when asked about the possibility of reopening the case, the chief commented, "*You're talking about a homicide suspect who has committed atrocious crimes.*" He further added, "*If you want to give any attribution to his ramblings on the Internet, go right ahead. But I do not.*"

When asked about Dorner's attempts to clear his name and set the records straight, the chief said that that simply was not going to happen.

The history of the LAPD has been especially fraught with tensions between the police force and the African American community both inside and outside the LAPD. Multiple times, people working inside the LAPD have insisted that racial discrimination was more than uncommon.

This coupled with the fact that shortly after Dorner's manifesto came to surface, the police opened fire on a car containing two Hispanic women raised a lot of alarms for everyone within the LAPD as people began to speculate whether the department simply made a lot of mistakes, or whether it really was as racially biased as they had been led to believe time and time again.

WARNING: SOME PHOTOS
MAY BE DISTURBING

PHOTOS

U.S. Reservist Chris Dorner

Dorner and Former LAPD Chief Wm. Bratton

Monica Quan, 28, the daughter of LAPD Captain Randal Quan and her fiance Keith Lawrence, 27

Riverside Police Officer Michael Crain gunned down by Dorner on Feb 7, 2013

Funeral of Officer Michael Crain

A Facebook post from Dorner claiming his innocence

Digital billboard LAPD Alert during the manhunt

San Bernardino Detective Jeremiah MacKay
killed by Dorner on Feb 12, 2013

Cabin in Big Bear, California on fire where Dorner was holed up inside

The cabin ruins after the fire

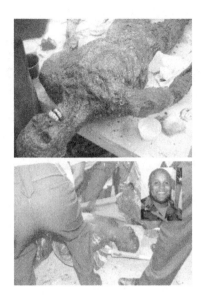

The supposed charred body of Dorner

Dorner's burnt-out truck at Big Bear

Mother and daughter's truck riddled with bullets

Another innocent citizen, rammed off the road and shot at by police

WHAT'S NEXT FOR THE LAPD?

The massive manhunt for former police officer Christopher J Dorner ended in a hail of bullets and a wall of flame as the mountain cabin he'd been hiding in caught fire after a brief cross-fire with the police. Two days later, the authorities confirmed that the body that had been recovered from the wreckage had belonged to Dorner.

"*The charred human remains located in the burned out cabin in Seven Oaks have been positively identified to be that of Christopher Dorner*," the San Bernardino County Sheriff-Coroner's Office said in a written statement. "*During the autopsy, positive identification was made through dental examination.*"

While Dorner's rampage is thankfully over, the repercussions for his actions have started to arise, and they are affecting the LAPD to the core as old animosities between the Department and the community it serves have started to rear their head.

The claims made by Dorner were bold and rather plain. In the 11,000 word manifesto he allegedly published on his Facebook page (though there are multiple accounts of the same manifesto now circulating the internet), Dorner stated that he had been discriminated against and had been deliberately driven out of the department for the simple crime of speaking up against the misconduct as he witnessed it committed by his training officer Teresa Evans.

He accused Evans of kicking a docile and bound suspect in the face twice. Issues of race and police brutality in relation with black people are not uncommon. Los Angeles is the city where the videotape of the police brutally beating black motorcyclist Rodney King first arose. What's more, the officers accused of beating the black man on video tape were later acquitted. This case caused multiple riots in 1992. The Department was also immersed in a flood of corruption charges and civil rights violations which later went on to be known as the Rampart Scandal. [6]

This scandal went on for the duration of the late 90s as well as the early 2000s. Eventually, this situation calmed down somewhat when the LAPD and the federal government sent an independent monitor to guide and enforce reforms.

Dorner stated in his manifesto that the situation had not changed a bit from the Rampart and Rodney King days but had in fact only gotten worse.

Dorner's words and the actions that followed from both sides poured a lot of salt in the wounds that had not healed completely in the black community of Los Angeles and had caused much damage to the Department's reputation already. The LAPD has a very long history of mistreating black people.

It wasn't until as late as the 1960s before the LAPD ended the forced segregation of squad cars. Now, Dorner's accusations have revived some not-so-savory ghosts who hadn't completely died out in the first place.

Experts state that on such a massive scale as this problem had been dealt with, there are bound to be aftershocks for many years to come.

A significant cause for alarm was the fact that callers on a local radio station that is popular in the African American community had been calling in on air and had been referring to Dorner as a hero, to the point that they even claimed that he would seek vengeance for the centuries worth of slavery that had been imposed on the black community. Furthermore, a Facebook page by the name of '*We Stand With Christopher Dorner*' had attracted more than 23,000 followers.

Dorner's supporters seem to have ignored the fact that he was supposedly a violent criminal because they see his rants not as the ravings of a lunatic but those of a man who had been oppressed by the system to the point that he set out to claim justice the only way he knew how: through force.

Though Dorner's approach to getting justice was wrong, it cannot be denied that the people who committed such racial atrocities against him, against innocent black men, against innocent and docile suspects are not any more right than the path Dorner chose. It makes a lot of people think that if this is the only way to get justice, just how old and bygone are the days old and gone by?

In an attempt to counter Dorner's resentments, the LAPD chief Charlie Beck announced that he had reopened Dorner's case. Beck stated that as hard as it had been to change the culture of the LAPD, it had been even harder to claim and maintain an air of trust inside the LAPD and between the LAPD and the public, and he would take every measure possible to maintain the air.

Therefore, Beck had continued, it is felt that the issue that has been brought to the public must be resolved in public as well. He said that this was the time to assure people that the LAPD was free and fair in all that it did. He said that he was not taking any steps to appease a murderer but to make sure that the public realized that no matter what anyone said, the police office was free and fair in all things it did.

The inquest is being taken as a sign that, despite whatever Dorner has to say, the department is trying to amend its ways and put its old days behind it.

Still, despite the fact that three civilians had been shot over mistaken identity and two of them has suffered gunshot wounds, the manhunt for Dorner had been rather successful, according to the LAPD. The huge task force that was assembled made sure that all agencies involved coordinated with each other, even though most of the agencies involved are generally not seen at such a crime scene, such as the Department of Fish and Wildlife. All resources, in short, were put to use so that there would be no chance that Dorner would be able to escape or harm anyone.

The LAPD, however, even years later is not willing to answer these questions about the possibility of a tarnished image and is still tight-lipped with the media. But in the end, even the people who might have agreed with Dorner did not agree with his message at all simply because of the fact that violence is never the correct approach to solving any problem, no matter which side it ensues from.

His explicit threats against the LAPD members and their families and even measures against some of the aforementioned were seen as barbaric acts of a lunatic.

Experts have commented time and time again that when someone goes after the families of the LAPD, it is seen as them going after the LAPD and the families of the institution, and then even the police start to take wrongful measures.

If there had ever been an opportunity for the LAPD to take measures to sort out the mess in which it currently is, it is now.

The LAPD's history has been riddled with racial crimes and especially crimes involving an excessive use of force against the suspects they have a duty to protect. This incident, especially, has set people's eyes on to the LAPD once again to see which move they will further make.

The LAPD can use this opportunity to make changes and amends in the system so that the people of Los Angeles are put at rest as well that racial discrimination in the LAPD is a thing of the past.

THE RACE FACTOR

Though it is true that Christopher Dorner is the last person on earth anyone should be idolizing, it is also true that we can no longer ignore the impact racism has on daily lives, even in high-end fields who are dedicated to stopping such crimes - the police departments.

To ignore Dorner's grievances just because of the method he chose would be quite a grave mistake. Between all the bloodshed and the diatribe, there is an opportunity here to strike while the iron is hot and take measures to lessen if not completely eradicate the racism that runs so deeply into the system.

If he had written his manifesto in the form of a testimony, he would have been offering what Critical Race Theorists would refer to as a Racial Battle Fatigue.

Racial Battle Fatigue [7] is a theory attributed to the psychological attrition that people of color face on an almost daily basis. This arises from the daily battle of deflecting racial insults, stereotypes and discrimination. It is the cumulative effect of being on guard and having to prepare responses to insults that are both subtle and overt.

This arsenal of quick wit and always being on the alert is known as self-protection from racial microaggressions and racialized aggression. RBF is mostly experienced by people of color who work in mostly 'white institutions'.

Within such institutions, people of color (non-white groups) have to deal with prejudices, discriminatory behavior and denigrating comments from people of any level and post, juniors and peers as well as seniors.

Racial microaggressions was a concept first used to describe only the sort of discriminatory behavior that people of color face in an academic institute or educational environment, but it is true and more than apparent that now the definition holds true elsewhere.

Indeed, it wouldn't be awry to say that racial microaggressions are a part of society at large. In order to understand the scope of Racial Battle Fatigue, we must first understand racial microaggressions.

Racial microaggressions are defined as:

- Subtle insults. Range from verbal insults to non-verbal insults and are directed at people of color. These are usually used automatically or unconsciously.

- Layered insults. Based on a person's race,

gender, class, sexuality, language, immigration status, accent or anything that might set them apart from what the society's norm of a white person is.

· Cumulative insults. Unnecessary stress that is layered on people of color while privileging white people.

In a daily environment, racial microaggressions take place all around us. Racial microaggressions are subtle remarks that the speaker often considers a compliment.

"You are not like other people of color."

"You don't look like a person of color."

"You speak English without an accent."

"You might be a person of color but you're not *like* them."

Racial microaggressions are part of a psychological warfare that is endured by people of color in environments that are heavy on the white population.

If you're wondering where Christopher Dorner comes into this scenario, some parts of his manifesto are a page straight out of the handbook of racial microaggressions against people of color (or would be if such a handbook existed.)

If Dorner's manifesto were to be used as raw data or something other than a criminal's game plan, one would proceed by tracing and highlighting through it, the racial themes that run throughout the whole tirade. In his manifesto, Dorner refers to two high-profile cases.

These are the Rampart Scandal and the Rodney King case both of which not only illuminated the grievances that people of color had and had been talking about for years, but also validated them. Both of these cases showed corruption in the police office to be a common occurrence.

The Rampart Scandal brought forth a whole culture of misconduct and the criminally casual abuse of authority by the LAPD, which included the false planting of evidence, using excessive force, dealing narcotics, robbing banks, as well as framing suspects for their own personal gains.

The Rodney King case in which the police were exposed using excessive use of force by viciously beating an unconscious man. An amateur videotape vividly exposed police brutality and effectively blew the LAPD's reputation to smithereens. "Serving and protecting" was revealed to be a big lie as images of cruelty and pure malice at the hands of the people's so-called protectors flooded the media.

One year after the Rodney King incident took place, the officers involved in the beating were acquitted. Minutes after the news of the decision acquitting them was broadcast, the unrest began in Los Angeles in the form of riots that later became to be known as the Los Angeles riots by the popular media.

This unrest was referred to by Critical Race Scholars as the Los Angeles Uprising of 1992. This uprising resulted in 53 deaths, thousands of injuries, and more than 6,000 incidents of fire. In solidarity with their Los Angeles brethren, San Francisco, Atlanta and Las Vegas also erupted into smaller scale uprisings.

Most of the mainstream popular newspapers stated that Dorner had a seemingly illogical and rather bottomless grudge against the LAPD when they fired him in 2009. Dorner had served for three years and stated in his manifesto that he had brought his grievances up the chain of command and had made them known to the higher-ups.

His grievances had been dismissed and he had been ultimately discharged. Dorner believed that he had been the victim of an act of revenge by the LAPD for crossing the 'Blue Line' which is an unspoken decree of secrecy between police officers.

Dorner had been portrayed by an ex-FBI profiler Jim Clemente as an "injustice collector". The reason behind this was that he held tight to detailed scenarios of what had happened, when and who did what to whom, and what the outcome of each scenario was.   He kept a record of racial microaggressions against not only himself but others as well. He cited those who had been victimized by the LAPD time and time again. These people included People of Color, the elderly, immigrants, the disabled, and hence everyone who was not in a particular position of power to defend themselves.

At some times, Dorner speaks in the character of a vigilante who is emerging from the shadows of injustice to right some wrongs. However, then he quickly crosses over to the dark side where he collects dead bodies as his severance.

According to researchers, the symptoms of Racial Battle Fatigue often include but are not limited to a loss of sense of control, insomnia, rapid mood swings, high blood pressure, ulcers and other symptoms that can be noticed in patients suffering from stress.

Stress from racial microaggressions can become rather lethal when the accumulation of physiological symptoms of Racial Battle Fatigue are left untreated, are not cared for properly, or are personally dismissed as is prone to happen in an environment where racial microaggressions are treated as a normal part of life and any voice raised against them is considered to be unnecessary noise.

This is particularly problematic as the sufferer may feel haunted by the fact that he thinks that his grievances are only imaginary. This can lead him to suffer from multiple mental health issues.

It is worth noting here that there are positive ways to dealing with the type of RBF Christopher Dorner suffered from. Being an educated man, Dorner could have dealt with his grief in a more productive way such as by going public, doing an expose, writing a book or even a screenplay depicting what he underwent and the type of activities that regularly go on inside the sacred LAPD.

He could even have staged a protest or a series of the same outside said police department. However, the minute he chose to fire the first shot, Dorner made a decision. He joined the circle of abuse and went from a victim to a predator, albeit on the other side of the line. His method of taking revenge effectively wiped out all the valid reasons he had for his frustration, and in the media that is far from unprejudiced itself, he got sidelined as his violence became the story.

By acting on his own sense of vengeance, Dorner has opened our eyes and shown us how each and every one of us is susceptible to participating in the cycle of abuse. When he was a rescuer, Dorner witnessed the abuse and incidents of usage of excessive force by his fellow officers and reported them in hopes to get some justice. In his manifesto, Dorner cites multiple counts of excessive use of unchecked power.

Dorner's manifesto was very informative in the sense that he had confronted each individual group for its actions or lack of actions and had cited the incidents as well as the responsibility of each group to stop it.

Joe Jones is another former LAPD Officer and a person of color. He countered Dorner's manifesto with one of his own where he pleaded with Dorner to stop killing innocent victims.

He made it rather clear that Dorner was not the first person to come across such a situation and hence he wasn't the only one with any grievances relating to the matter.

He made an appeal to the citizens of Los Angeles, the government, the politicians and both to the honest and dishonest members of the LAPD, as well as to Dorner himself. He said that he himself had suffered for no less than eighteen years. He calls these eighteen years of psychological strain, self-doubt and torment.

Many people of color who suffer at the hands of their superiors do so in silence. At most, the suffering is discussed with a small circle of family and friends because confronting the perpetrators of racial microaggressions or even speaking up about them comes with a risk.

The first of these risks is that you will not be believed or will be told that you are not the first to suffer as such and thus should remain silent about it, the second that you will be discredited, and the third that you will be blamed for initiating something yourself.

Out of these, the most damaging, perhaps, is the option that you will be silenced by inaction.

Even more, by speaking about them, silencing by in-action makes a person believe that their words do not matter and that their grievances are imaginary at best.

MANHUNT – ERIC FREIN IN COMPARISON WITH CHRIS DORNER

Let's discuss a rogue police murderer of this era - Eric Frein. [8] After a massive 48-day manhunt, three deputy US Marshals saw the accused cop killer 'moving through tall grass' and yet they 'could see his hands and see that he was not carrying any sort of weapons.'

Frein was taken into custody near an airport hangar without any sort of incident whatsoever. This was completely different from the Christopher Dorner manhunt which resulted in a shootout and, ultimately, Dorner's death. This situation was also different from the confrontation and detention of the jaywalker Mike Brown in Ferguson. This also was unlike the detention and capture of the "reasonably suspicious" Ezell Ford in Los Angeles.

Officers in the police force are taught that time is on their side, there is no need to rush in and that the suspect can always be waited out. Since this is a part of the official training, one could claim that this is the official protocol the LAPD and San

Bernardino Sheriff had to follow after they had surrounded the cabin where Christopher Dorner had been hiding.

The question arises, why were both departments in such a hurry that they couldn't even wait a full twenty-four or even twelve hours? What was the urgency here?

It had been reported that Dorner had been spotted in different places leading up to the cabin several times during the 9-day manhunt and had escaped the authorities every time much like Eric Frein.

Why did Ferguson's police officer Darren Wilson need to confront Mike Brown in the middle of the street and why couldn't he wait until Brown had crossed over to the sidewalk?

And what was so important a topic that a gang of LAPD officers needed to talk to Ezell Ford about that they had to confront him and initiate a struggle that ultimately ended in his death? And couldn't this "talk" wait for another day or be held in another, less lethal way?

Eric Frein had been described as a survivalist with an extensive shooting background. He was someone with a grudge against law enforcement, someone who had premeditated over the murders he had been hoping to commit.

He had been preparing for them for months, if not years, before. Frein had been named as one of the FBI's top ten most wanted criminals, and yet he was considered to be less frightening to the law enforcement officials than Dorner, Ford or even the jaywalker Brown.

It had been reported that Frein had left or abandoned an AK-47 and ammunition as well as two pipe bombs, and they had been used as bread crumbs for the pursuing officers to discover.

However, in the matter of Frein, there were no accusations of 'scaring the police', no hiding of the hands and no reaching for the waistband. Not a flash bang had been thrown and no structures had been burnt to the ground once Frein had been spotted. Reports revealed that as soon as Frein had been spotted with his guard down, he had simply been ordered to lie face down, to which he obliged, and was later handcuffed.

There are some interesting similarities between the Christopher Dorner manhunt and the Eric Frein manhunt except for the little technical detail that Dorner had been black while Frein had been white. Frein and Dorner both had given a lot of thought to their attacks.

Both had been called armed and dangerous and both were reported to be exceptionally good shooters. Both of them allegedly killed law enforcement officials in a cold-blooded and calculated manner, and yet only one of them had been told to lie face down and had been handcuffed.

Though neither Frein's nor Dorner's actions are commendable or condoned, the apparent disparity between the way police officers treat or rather 'handle' black/brown people and white people is bothering, to say the least.

Brown or black people are not mythological creatures to be feared. They are not dragons who can only be confronted and tackled in unfair ways because they somehow have some sort of advantage over a person. What was the urgency in taking down Christopher Dorner that the police had to burn a cabin to the ground?

Additionally, what were the special circumstances that precipitated the Mike Brown Shooting? What was so scary about Ezell Ford's actions? If Eric Frein can be hunted for more than forty days in relentless pursuit and can be brought down in a non-lethal way and can be captured peacefully, should that not be the norm as to how this sort of a situation should be dealt with every time around?

There might be a lot of red tape around the capture of Frein as most of the details are still yet unknown to public. However, the fact that a serial cop killer can be given the chance to come in quietly and that a black man in South Carolina can be shot when he reaches for the driver's license a patrol officer asked for is rather alarming.

A passenger in Hammond, Indiana was ordered to show his identification and was tasered and arrested when he failed to show it. The coroner in Oklahoma ruled the death of a black man a homicide after officers struggled with him in a movie theater, and yet most of the culprits of these crimes, men and women in uniforms, got fined or a light tap on the back of their hands at the most, while Frein is still alive and innocent black men are dead.

A FORENSIC OUTLOOK

It would be a crass attempt at stating the obvious to say that Christopher Dorner was an extremely angry man. Mass murderers are almost always frustrated and angry to a certain degree about something.

This could be work, love, life, finances, social status, the loss of something or someone special, failure to attain grandiose fantasies, a lack of self-recognition or acceptance of self or someone else, feelings of being persecuted, rejection, childhood trauma, or anything that can have a long-term effect on someone's psychology.

And there is often a significant grain of truth in their wrath against reality. There is often a comprehensible and somewhat understandable reason to be furious about their lives. There are two distinguishing factors in the Christopher Dorner case that set it apart from other cases about mass murderers and even other cops that have gone rogue.

The first is the fact that Dorner was someone who had been a former police officer. He was the typical good cop gone bad who started angrily assassinating not only former colleagues but also their families. The other is the racial component where Mr. Dorner was an African-American who believed that he had been the victim of racial discrimination. Dorner believed that, in part, he had been fired due to the color of his skin.

If you take a look at the Facebook note off Dorner's profile, which later went on to become his manifesto, he alleges the LAPD of being racist, and that is not without historical precedent.

And despite the fact that this problem had been present in the system for a long time, it had still not been eradicated completely and had resulted in the sort of psychological stress and damage caused by it as we witnessed in Christopher Dorner's case.

Indeed, it is only now, after the damage has been done and Dorner himself has left this life, that his case is being reopened to review whether Dorner's initial claims of cover-up and racial discrimination had held any merit at all. It still remains to be seen if Dorner's claims of race playing a significant part in his 2008 dismissal are correct or not, and the truth is, that is something we may never find out.

Regardless of whatever the outcome of that new investigation turns out to be, truth is that mass shooters like Dorner always have some festering grievance against the world, whether it be related to ethnicity, gender, race, religion, romance, politics, economics, status or any other reason.

And like most people are prone to do, these mass murderers heap all their ire, resentment, bitterness and discontent onto the one factor or factors they believe to be responsible for their bad luck, neglect, suffering, humiliation, loss or mistreatment; be it parents, the government, teachers, spouses, bosses, technology, Wall Street or just society at large.

Apparently the thing that infuriated Christopher Dorner the most was the fact that he was losing position as a police officer, and that in his own eyes was equivalent to losing his good name or reputation.

In his bitter tirade online which later went on to be his manifesto, Dorner recalled the cases of Ted Kaczynski, the Unabomber and Norwegian mass murderer Anders Breivik. He reminisced about his childhood in Southern California and recounted that he grew up in an almost exclusively Caucasian neighborhood and school.

He mentions that his first encounter with racism was early in his childhood. He further describes how this racism followed him all his life and only increased during his brief time serving in the LAPD.

He believed that it was this racism, along with the unspoken thin blue line that bonds police departments in professional camaraderie and yet strongly discourages reporting bad behavior in any fellow police officer that led to his unfair dismissal from the officer, after he not only witnessed but formally documented the unfair use of cruel and excessive force by a senior training police officer during the arrest of a mentally ill person.

Judging from most accounts, Christopher Dorner held himself and most others to a high moral standard, especially the police force who he thoroughly believed to be protectors rather than perpetrators.

Dorner was especially sensitive to and was aggressively vocal about racial discrimination. Judging from his manifesto, it was quite a disillusionment for Dorner to realize that such hurtful racism not only still lingers in the LAPD but also runs freely and affects people on a daily basis.

Here, countering this argument with the fact that America has not only elected but has also re-elected an African American as its president and to consider it equivalent to the eradication of racism in America is not only ludicrous but also rather delusional a thing to claim.

If we were to discuss the issue of racism, rage and mass murder, another case comes to mind, and that is the one of Colin Ferguson in New York City. In 1993, Ferguson who was a black man born and raised in Jamaica, calmly boarded a Long Island Rail Road car during rush hour commute and started shooting people.

This resulted in five deaths and eighteen people being wounded. Ferguson did not try to commit suicide as many other mass murderers are prone to do, either out of an embittered sense of despair, rage, hopelessness or in order to avoid having to face the consequences for the act they committed.

Not all mass murderers are suicidal, wanting to stick around and bask in the notoriety and infamy relished by their rage for recognition. In fact, many of them actively enjoy the chaos and suffering they create.

Looking at it from a traditional point of view, many mass murderers single out and target specific victims or at least victims that fit a specific profile, such as spouses, lovers, family members, co-workers, employees and the like, towards whom they wish to seek revenge to repay for some perceived or actual insult.

Others such as Seung Hui Cho at Virginia Tech, accused Batman shooter James Holmes in Colorado, and Anders Breivik in Norway make premeditated and meaningful choices about where, when and how to commit their crimes and don't care much about who the victim is as long as someone is unfortunate enough to be present there.

For example, once he was aboard the train, Ferguson's victims were selected more or less on impulse and haphazardly. Dorner's victims, on the other hand, were specifically listed and staked out and targeted.

He was waging quite skilled guerilla warfare against the individuals whom he believed had wronged him somehow. He was also going after their families as is apparent by the fact that he executed his defense counsel Ronald Quan's daughter, Monica Quan, along with her fiancé in their car.

He also targeted former Los Angeles police officers at large. Though he had ample opportunity to kill other individuals who were not related to law enforcement, he had chosen not to do so.

In this sense, the two crimes committed by Colin Ferguson and Christopher Dorner were rather different; however, both of these men had apparently been deeply wounded by the unfair system that put more weight in racism than it did in individuals.

Both these men, in short, had been disappointed by the system: Ferguson upon arriving in America as a naïve young man from his more privileged upbringing in Jamaica as well as Dorner who grew up in a predominantly white environment in Southern California and purportedly later as a rookie police officer in Los Angeles.

Both of these men were extremely frustrated and angry and felt tormented by their unfair fate. Both had allowed their rage to stew for some time.

This period of stewing or festering is typically present in a mass murderer and can last from days to decades. It also makes up a key factor leading up to and driving their violent outbursts.

This can be regarded as a tragic example of what most people call chronic anger mismanagement. This anger mismanagement led both men to exact hateful and violent revenge on those they felt had wronged them, had impeded their progress in life or had stood in their way somehow.

Colin Ferguson, who was deemed to be depressed and psychotic at the time of the shootings, deliberately targeted middle-class Caucasians on a commuter train because they had been strangers who had been representatives of the 'American Dream' for him, a dream which he had never had for himself, and thus he deemed his victims the cause of his personal frustration, failure and disillusionment. He violently victimized the people he felt were victimizers.

Dorner was also likely depressed and embittered but not psychotic like Colin Ferguson. He had served as a former Navy reservist prior to joining the LAPD and had directly declared war on his former brethren who he had felt had betrayed and destroyed his life. Dorner was out for blood and retribution.

However, according to his own words, Christopher Dorner's motivation transcended mere revenge. His motivation was driven by a compulsive need to set the record straight, right a wrong and clear his name.

In his manifesto, he goes on about the meaning and importance of having a good name, of having a professional reputation, and the devastating effects of having his worth in life sullied and tarnished simply because of unfair racial practices.

This is something that concerns almost every human being at some point in their life because it is an existential fact of life that a person seldom possesses anything of worth other than his good name. And to have that hard-earned reputation and good name taken from you in the blink of an eye is something that can cause anyone to have a meltdown, especially if your name was tarnished over something as cruel as racial inequality.

Despite our best efforts to keep our reputations intact, we are all potentially susceptible to such a cataclysmic loss of what we hold so dear, precious and meaningful to us in our life. None of us can say with any certainty how dear our name is to us and how we would react to such a profound sort of existential crisis of losing said name and especially when the reason is, at least in some parts, unfair, unjust and the product of racial discrimination.

Racism is rooted in a fundamental fear and a defensive sort of resentment and hostility towards those we project our 'rejected' shadow upon.

Due to our conditioning, more than anything else, our mind believes that the people we are being racist towards are somehow beneath us and are thus somehow rejected. We deem these people as 'others' and deem them different and inferior.

The demonic rage, racial animus and plain hatred that accompany these sentiments are the few social evils that America still faces, and these are the social evils that seem to be the most deeply rooted in society. However, here arises a crucial question of how someone, no matter who they are, black, white, brown, Muslim, Hindu, Jew, anyone, deals with such self-evident evils as well as the frustration, anger, and rage they are bound to provoke.

Colin Ferguson found his few remaining shreds of meaning after his world had been blown more or less away in hating white people whom he saw as prejudicially thwarting his way to economic success in the country, especially success he may have felt narcissistically entitled to.

This behavior is not uncommon in xenophobes as well as members of the KKK. The reason behind this is that it is always easier to blame someone else for our problems, anger and failure than to face the music, as the term goes. From Ferguson's perspective, his victims symbolized the devils and the villains who had been, in his eyes, victimizing him all along.

Similarly, the righteous indignation that was

showed by Chris Dorner about being dismissed by the LAPD somehow twisted itself into the shape of a one-man crusade to clean up the residual racism that still ran amok in the offices of the LAPD. However, even more meaningful and important than to clean up the department had been the point of clearing his ruined reputation as a good police officer.

"I have exhausted all available means at obtaining my name back. I have attempted all legal court efforts within appeals at the Superior Courts and California Appellate courts. This is my last resort." It seems that Dorner had always wanted to be a policeman and that his self-esteem and sense of meaning and purpose in life had been closely linked to having finally attained this dream.

Of course, when that dream shattered, Dorner's violent reign of terror became his sole sense of power as well as his biggest sense of purpose in life, i.e. it was the one thing that kept him going. Dorner was undoubtedly deeply wounded by his treatment by the department and had written in his manifesto that he admitted that he had fallen into a deep state of severe depression after he had been fired.

In any case, it is almost confirmed that what happened to Dorner had been a massive narcissistic injury that had resulted in the immense narcissistic rage of the wounded. Psychoanalyst Heinz Kohut (1978) defines narcissistic rage as *"The need for re-*

venge, for righting a wrong, for undoing a hurt by whatever means, and a deeply anchored, unrelenting compulsion in the pursuit of all of these aims, which give no rest to those who have suffered a narcissistic injury-- these are the characteristic features of narcissistic rage in all its forms and which sets it apart from other kinds of aggression."

Here arises the question of whether Dorner met the profile for Narcissistic Personality Disorder. The answer to that is: not necessarily. Dorner had been reportedly bullied as a child and had been hurt and angered by racial taunts.

The general impression one gets of Christopher Dorner from reading his manifesto, watching interviews of the people who were close to him such as girlfriends, family, friends and co-workers is that Dorner had been a sensitive and idealistic person.

He was somewhat rigid and one could go far as to say dogmatic in his sense of right and wrong. His ex-girlfriend reported that there had been phases where Dorner went between being 'good Chris' and 'bad Chris.' This can be easily pinpointed into being something that Carl Jung calls a shadow or a person's dark side which exists in everyone but does not manifest dominantly in a lot of people.

Of course, it was something that manifested itself dominantly in Dorner himself as was evident by his fury and the path he took himself later on in life. At the end, it seems that Dorner had become a man of high moral and principles who had been unable to come to grips with his own raging demons of resentment.

He had been someone who felt victimized by evil but, lacking any constructive solution, had taken the path of fighting evil with evil and fire with fire. When we take a look at the manifesto, we see Dorner describe his actions as a necessary evil and thus come to the conclusion that he, like many other serial killers and mass murderers, had been in a dangerous state of mind for a period of time prior to his killing spree.

Calling his actions a necessary evil hints upon the fact that until the very end, Dorner had been well aware of what is right and what is wrong and had been able to differentiate between good and evil himself.

As has been witnessed in the cases of Colin Ferguson, Adam Lanza, Anders Breivik and other mass murderers or serial killers, Dorner could find no way out of the problem he found himself in, at least no productive way. Dorner could not contend with his frustration, disillusionment, anger and rage constructively and did not seek any professional help to get him through the ordeal either, as far as records tell us.

It is a sad fact that denying or repressing rage only tends to intensify it over a period of time which makes it all the more dangerous. The tragic result in both cases is a catastrophic detonation of destructive violence, and even though violence is not the answer in any way, it can be understood as an eruption of pent-up passion, an explosion of the drive to destroy what can be seen as the barrier to a person's self-esteem, movement and growth.

No one is immune to anger and almost everyone is susceptible to feelings of rage, anger and violent fantasies that usually accompany such dark thoughts. However, what differentiates between the majority of the world and the likes of Colin Ferguson, Seung Hui Cho, Anders Breivik, Adam Lanza or the Christopher Dorners of the world is the fact that a majority of us do not, as Shakespeare put it in Hamlet, 'take arms against a sea of troubles.' Of course, this is the last desperate stance of the troubled and embittered mass shooter.

In conclusion, the fact to be emphasized is that all of these murderers did not wake up one day and decide to kill every white person they saw. Behind these people is a history of oppression, both on a small and personal scale as well as on a larger and more historical perspective.

Dorner grew up in the midst of a white-heavy environment and thus became exposed to racial bullying at a very young age, and from a very young age, his mind had been exposed to hate since children of color are usually the first victims of bullying in any environment, especially one where the white population is heavier and greater in numbers. The whole Christopher Dorner saga could have been well avoided had the system been accustomed to checks and balances on every scale that makes sure that racial prejudice gets stopped and ultimately eradicated.

The thing to remember is that, in the end, Dorner did not get even a small percentage of the reward he had set out to get. He died in infamy and his retaliatory tactics did not redeem his reputation as he had hoped they would. In fact, he had completely destroyed his reputation long before his death because even if he had not been a liar, he had become a killer.

Here arises the question of whether his death will play any part in the reformation and improvement of the LAPD as he had allegedly intended in the first place. There is some hope that the police will learn a lesson from this and will learn to set aside racial prejudices whilst handling criminals or even potential criminals.

The LAPD has a long history of both racial discrimination and excessive use of force against the people it is supposed to be serving, and this is as good an opportunity as any to make amends.

Enjoy this book? You can make a big difference.

Reviews are one of the most powerful tools when it comes to book ranking, exposure and future sales. I have a bunch of loyal readers and honest reviews of my books help bring them to the attention of other readers.

If you've enjoyed this book, I would be very grateful if you'd take a few minutes to write a brief review on Amazon.

Thank you so much
RJ

OTHER BOOKS BY RJ PARKER

Parents Who Killed Their Children: True stories of Filicide, Mental Health and Postpartum Psychosis

Serial Homicide: Notorious Serial Killers: (4 Books in Series)

Abduction

Top Cases of the FBI: Volumes I and II

The Basement

Forensic Analysis and DNA in Criminal Investigations and Cold Cases Solved: True Crime Stories

Serial Killers Encyclopedia: The Encyclopedia of Serial Killers from A to Z

Social Media Monsters: Killers Who Target Victims on the Internet

Escaped Killer

Revenge Killings

Killing the Rainbow

Marc Lépine: True Story of the Montreal Massacre: School Shootings

Backseat Tragedies: Hot Car Deaths

Women Who Kill

Beyond Stick and Stones

Cold Blooded Killers

Case Closed: Serial Killers Captured

Radical Islamic Terrorist in America Today

Hell's Angels Biker War

Serial Killer Groupies

Serial Killer Case Files

Blood Money: The Method and Madness of Assassins: Stories of Real Contract Killers

Serial Killers True Crime Anthologies: Volumes 1 - 4

ABOUT THE AUTHOR

RJ Parker, PhD, is an award-winning and best-selling true crime author and owner of RJ Parker Publishing, Inc. He has written over 30 true crime books which are available in eBook, paperback and audiobook editions and have sold in over 100 countries. He holds certifications in Serial Crime, Criminal Profiling and a PhD in Criminology.

To date, RJ has donated over 3,000 autographed books to allied troops serving overseas and to our wounded warriors recovering in Naval and Army hospitals all over the world. He also donates to Victims of Violent Crimes Canada.

If you are a police officer, firefighter, paramedic or serve in the military, active or retired, RJ gives his eBooks freely in appreciation for your service.

CONTACT INFORMATION

Bookbub:

rjpp.ca/BOOKBUB-RJPARKER

Author's Email:

AuthorRJParker@gmail.com

Publisher's Email:

Agent@RJParkerPublishing.com

Website:

http://m.RJPARKERPUBLISHING.com/

Twitter:

http://www.Twitter.com/realRJParker

Facebook:

https://www.facebook.com/RJParkerPublishing

Amazon Author's Page:

rjpp.ca/RJ-PARKER-BOOKS

THE BASEMENT

On March 24, 1987, the Philadelphia Police Department received a phone call from a woman who stated that she had been held captive for the last four months. When police officers arrived at the pay phone from which the call was made, Josefina Rivera told them that she and three other women had been held captive in a basement by a man named Gary Heidnik. This is a shocking story of kidnapping, rape, torture, mutilation, dismemberment, decapitation, and murder.

The subject matter in this book is graphic

http://rjpp.ca/THE-BASEMENT

Available in eBook, Paperback and Audiobook editions

SERIAL KILLERS ENCYCLOPEDIA

The ultimate reference for anyone compelled by the pathology and twisted minds behind the most disturbing of homicidal monsters. From A to Z, and from around the world, these serial killers have killed in excess of 3,000 innocent victims, affecting thousands of friends and family members. There are monsters in this book that you may not have heard of, but you won't forget them after reading their case. This reference book will make a great collection for true crime aficionados.

http://bit.ly/SK-ENCYCLOPEDIA

Available in eBook, Paperback and Audiobook editions

PARENTS WHO KILLED THEIR CHILDREN

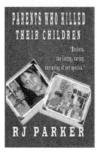

What could possibly incite parents to kill their own children?

This collection of "filicidal killers" provides a gripping overview of how things can go horribly wrong in once-loving families. Parents Who Killed Their Children depicts ten of the most notorious and horrific cases of homicidal parental units out of control. People like Andrea Yates, Diane Downs, Susan Smith, and Jeffrey MacDonald who received a great deal of media attention. The author explores the reasons, from addiction to postpartum psychosis, insanity to altruism.

Each story is detailed with background information on the parents, the murder scenes, trials, sentencing and aftermath.

http://bit.ly/PARENTSWHOKILLED

Available in eBook, Paperback and Audiobook editions

BLOOD MONEY: THE METHOD AND MADNESS OF ASSASSINS

From the old days of mobsters in smoky barrooms plotting to gun down their rivals, to the new age of ordinary people hiring contract killers through the Dark Web, this book depicts the history of assassins and how they work.

While movies portray assassins as glamorous, wealthy and full of mystery, the sober truth is often quite different.

The number of homicides credited to contract killers each year is staggering, and on the rise: business people killing their rivals, organized gang war kills, honor killings and even cold-blooded kills between spouses.

In *Blood Money: The Method and Madness of Assassins*, RJ Parker documents over a dozen infamous cases of professional assassins including Richard

Kuklinski (The Ice Man), Charles Harrelson (Natural Born Killer) and Vincent Coll (Mad Dog).

Blood Money

Available in eBook, Paperback and Audiobook editions

[1]

http://www.policebrutality.info/2014/03/cops-who-shot-inno-cent-women-will-be-sent-back-into-field.html

[2] https://en.wikipedia.org/wiki/Christopher_Dorner_shootings_and_manhunt

[3] http://murderpedia.org/male.D/d/dorner-christopher.htm

[4] https://factreal.wordpress.com/2013/02/08/manifesto-of-cop-killer-chris-dorners-full-text/

[5] http://www.democraticunderground.com/101655176

[6] http://www.pbs.org/wgbh/pages/frontline/shows/lapd/scandal/

[7] https://www.researchgate.net/profile/William_Smith57/publication/247752199_Assume_the_Position_._._._You_Fit_the_DescriptionPsychosocial_Experiences_and_Racial_Battle_Fatigue_Among_African_American_Male_College_Students/links/54ef02da0cf2e55866f3daf4.pdf

[8] http://www.latimes.com/nation/la-na-frein-man-hunt-20141027-story.html

Made in the USA
Monee, IL
27 August 2021